OUT OF MANY, ONE PEOPLE

THE STORY OF
JAMAICA
ILLUSTRATED

Words and paintings by
KAVION ROBINSON
www.kavionart.com
Edited by: Kerice Robinson

About Artist

My name is Kavion Robinson I am an Illustrator and painter, recognized most notably for my illustrative paintings of historical figures. I was born in Jamaica. I moved to the United States as a teen. I attended the University of The Arts in Philadelphia, where I earned my bachelor of fine arts in 2009. My artistic style can be described as conceptual realism, sometimes a bit surreal in the concepts. Growing up in Jamaica, I saw a lot of beauty and struggle all at the same time. What I did not see growing up in Jamaica are paintings of people that looked like me in the history books. As a painter, I made it my goal to paint images of cultural and historical significance. I have dedicated my career as an artist to depict black life in an enlightening and educational manner. I received several awards for my paintings, most notable for excellence in figure painting from the National Gallery of Jamaica in 2012 for my historical oil paintings of several of Jamaica's national heroes. As an illustrator, I have illustrated several children's books most notable Irie the Butterfly and Irie the Caterpillar. My upbringing thought me to take great pride in my culture and history. That sense of cultural pride shines thru in my paintings. Especially this current body of work and historical picture book Out of Many, One People: *The story of Jamaica Illustrated.*

Thank you!

I would like to thank all those who motivated me to create Out of Many: *my grandparents; my parents, Maxine and Daniel Robinson; my sisters, Kerika and Kerice Robinson; my nieces, cousins, and my godson Kyle who I aim to inspire with this book. A huge thank-you to my editor Kerice Robinson. A very special thank-you to leaders, authors, and creators whose life and works inspired my love of history, namely Rt. Hon. Marcus Mosiah Garvey Sr. and Rt. Hon. Dr. Louise Bennett Coverley (Miss Lou).*

Out of Many, One People : The story of Jamaica Illustrated

Copyright©2019 by Kavion Robinson

Written, Illustrated, Designed by Kavion Robinson

All image rights reserved. Kavionart
www.kavionart.com

Prologue

Most people my age do not speak much about the past. For some, they simply don't see the importance of history. For others, it may just be too hard to relive a history filled with pain, struggle, slavery, and mass murder. I found pictures to be an inspirational way to preserve history and spark conversation. Growing up I did not see many images that piqued my interest to learn more about Jamaica, its people, and rich history. It motivated me to paint images that depict Jamaica's past and present in an inspiring manner. I dedicated my career as an artist to painting images of black people and black culture in an enlightening and educational manner.

The National Anthem

Eternal Father bless our land,
Guard us with Thy Mighty Hand,
Keep us free from evil powers,
Be our light through countless hours.
To our Leaders, Great Defender,
Grant true wisdom from above.
Justice, Truth be ours forever,
Jamaica, Land we love.
Jamaica, Jamaica, Jamaica land we love.

Teach us true respect for all,
Stir response to duty's call, strengthen us the weak to cherish,
Give us vision lest we perish.
Knowledge send us Heavenly Father,
Grant true wisdom from above.
Justice, Truth be ours forever,
Jamaica, land we love.
Jamaica, Jamaica, Jamaica land we love.

Written by Rev. Hon. Hugh Sherlock, composed by Hon. Robert Lightbourne, and arranged by Mapletoft Poulle and Christine Alison Poulle.

Rev. Hon. Hugh Sherlock
b. March 21, 1905 - d. April 19, 1998

National Pledge

Before God and all mankind, I pledge the love and loyalty of my heart, the wisdom and courage of my mind, the strength and vigour of my body in the service of my fellow citizens; I promise to stand up for Justice, Brotherhood and Peace, to work diligently and creatively, to think generously and honestly, so that Jamaica may, under God, increase in beauty, fellowship and prosperity, and play her part in advancing the welfare of the whole human race.

NATIVE ISLANDERS

Arawak Princess (Xaymaca 1494)

Xaymaca (Jamaica), the land of wood & water was filled with beautiful strong native islanders. The Caribbean was inhabited by Arawaks and Tiano Indians long before the arrival of the Spaniards. The arrival of Christopher Columbus in 1494 brought enslavement, rape, deadly diseases, and mass murder to shores of Xaymaca. Only a few Arawaks that managed to escape into the mountains and neighboring islands survived.

With the death of the Caribbean natives, the Europeans kidnapped and trafficked enslaved African men, women, and children to the Caribbean during the transatlantic slave trade.

NATIONAL HEREOS : *The Fight For Freedom*

"I would rather die upon yonders gallows than live my life in slavery." -Samuel Sharpe

Queen Nanny or Nanny of the Maroons
(c. 1680s – c. 1760s)

The arrival of African slaves to Jamaica brought a young Asante girl that grew to be a fierce warrior and freedom fighter. The mother of Jamaica as we know it today. We call her Nanny, Queen Nanny, and Nanny of the Maroons. Nanny was a frequent runaway slave, after multiple attempts she successfully escaped with a group of slaves which included her three brothers Accompong, Cudjoe, and Quao. They ran deep into the Blue Mountains where they formed small communities in Saint James and Saint Elizabeth. They became Maroons, Maroon was a term used for Africans and their descendants in the Americas and Caribbean who formed settlements away from the plantations. Cudjoe became the leader of the Leeward Maroons in the west. Nanny led the Windward Maroons in the east.

The Maroons led multiple slave rebellions and plantation raids, which led to the First Maroon War in the early 1730s. Nanny and Captain Cudjoe would agree to peace treaties in 1739 and 1740 with the British colonizers in exchange for land. The Maroons also agreed to help the British troops in battle against invaders.

Nanny is credited with freeing over a thousand slaves. Not much is known about her death. Many believe Nanny lived to be an old woman who died of natural causes in the 1750s and is buried in New Nanny Town (Moore Town). Jamaica declared Queen Nanny a National Heroin in 1975.

NATIONAL HEREOS : *The Fight For Freedom*

Rt. Excellent Samuel Sharpe
(1801 - May 23, 1832)

Samuel Sharpe was born into slavery on a plantation in the parish of St. James owned by Samuel and Jane Sharpe. His last name Sharpe is that of the plantation owner. His exact date of birth is unknown but his age at death in 1832 was listed as 31 making 1801 the year of his birth. Sharpe became a well-known preacher and leader in the Baptist Church. He was sent from plantation to plantation preaching to the slaves. Samuel used that freedom to travel and meet with other slaves. During these meetings, he was able to organize the largest and longest slave rebellion in Jamaica's history.

The Christmas Rebellion (Baptist War) began on the 27th of December 1831 at the Kensington Estate. It began as a peaceful protest until armed British forces and plantation workers clashed with slaves. The rebellion lasted 10 days across the different plantations, some 14 whites died compared to the over 200 black slaves that lost their lives. In the aftermath, Sharpe was captured and hanged in 1832 along with over 300 others who participated in the rebellion.

The rebellion led to multiple investigations into the conditions of slavery in the Caribbean. It contributed to the decision by Parliament in 1833 to pass the Slavery Abolition Act. Slavery was abolished across all British colonies in 1838. The Montego Bay location where Samuel Sharpe was executed was renamed Sam Sharpe Square in his honor. In 1975, the Jamaican government proclaimed Samuel Sharpe a National Hero.

Kavion Robinson
Martyrdom of Sam Sharpe, 2011
Oil on paper, 12 x16 in

NATIONAL HEREOS : *The Fight For Freedom*

Rt. Excellent Paul Bogle
(b. 1820 – d. Oct. 24, 1865)

Paul Bogle was a Baptist deacon and activist in St. Thomas. Bogle became a deacon of the Stony Gut Baptist Church in 1864 with help of wealthy landowner and fellow Baptist George William Gordon. Bogle became extremely focused on improving the living conditions of the poor. In 1864 he led a small group of farmers 45 miles to the capital, Spanish Town to express their graveness to Governor Eyre but was dined a meeting with the Governor.

On the 7th of October 1865, Bogle and others marched to the courthouse in support of two men from Stony Gut that were on trial for trespassing on a long-abandoned plantation. The police confronted the group in front of the courthouse and it turned violent. By Monday, October 9th, 1865, warrants were issued for Bogle and his supporters' arrest. On October 11th, 1865, Bogle led hundreds of followers to the courthouse. The police had organized a volunteer militia that fired into the group of protestors sparking a clash that led to over 20 deaths. Bogle and his supporters took control of the parish for two days.

Governor Eyre declared martial law. Troops were sent into Stony Gut to end the unrest. The troops killed over 400 people including women and children. Bogle and over 300 others were captured and arrested. Bogle was tried under martial law and quickly executed on October 24th 1865. Governor Eyre was recalled to England and eventually dismissed for ordering the mass executions. In 1969 Paul Bogle was named a National Hero of Jamaica.

NATIONAL HEREOS : *The Fight For Freedom*

George William Gordon
(b. 1820 - d. 1865)

George William Gordon was a mixed-race landowner, businessman, and politician. His father was a Scottish planter, Joseph Gordon and mother a salve woman, Ann Rattray. Gordon was very outspoken about the suffering of the poor, the oppression, and discrimination by the upper-class. He was elected in St. Thomas East parish as a member of the House of Assembly. Gordon established a Baptist church in Stony Gut and named Paul Bogle deacon. Gordon would help Bogle organize marches for better living conditions for the poor blacks. These marches led to the Morant Bay Rebellion of 1865. After Bogle and others were arrested and executed, Governor Eyre ordered the arrest of Gordon, whom he suspected of helping to plan the rebellion. Gordon was tried for high treason, sentenced to death, and executed on the 23rd of October 1865.

In 1938 the play *George William Gordon* by Roger Mais was written about Gordon's life. In 1960 the Parliament of Jamaica established the new Gordon House in his honor. In 1969, the Jamaican government proclaimed George William Gordon a National Hero of Jamaica.

The Negro World

The Indispensable Weekly — The Voice of the Awakened Negro

Reaching the Mass of Ne — The Best Advertising Medium

A N— Devoted Solely to the Interests of the Negro Race

VOL. XX. No. 25 — TURDAY, JULY 31, 1928 — HON. MARCUS GARVEY, NY. O—

GREAT WOR— —TION OF NEGROE—

Leaders for the Negro People of —— —claration of Rights of the Negro Peoples of the Wo—

In order to encourage our race —
to stimulate it to a higher and gra— —
and insist on the following Decla— —

1. "Be it known to all men —
created equal and entitled to the —
the pursuit of happiness, and b— —
elected representatives of the N— —
invoking the aid of the jus— —
all men, women and — —
world free citizens, and — —
Africa, the Motherland of —

2. "That we believe in t— —
race in all things racial; that —
given to men as a common poste— —
be an equitable distribution and app— —
things, and in consideration of the f— —
are now deprived of those things th— —
legally ours, we believe it right that a— —
be acquired and held by whatsoever —

3. That we believe the Negro —
should be governed by the ethics — —
therefore, should not be deprived of any o— —
privileges common to other human beings."

4. We declare that Negroes, wheresoever —
community among themselves, should be g— —
to elect their own representatives to repr— —
legislatures, courts of law, or such instit— —
exercise control over that particular comm— —

5. We assert that the Negro is entitled t— —
justice before all courts of law and equity —
country he may be found, and when this is d— —
account of his race or color such denial is an i— —
race as a whole and should be resented by the en— —
of Negroes."

6. "We declare it unfair and prejudicial to the —
of Negroes in communities where they exist in consi— —
able numbers to be tried by a judge and jury compo— —
entirely of an alien race, but in all such cases m— —
of our race are entitled to representation on the —

23. "We declare it inhuman and unfair to b— Negroes from industries and labor in any part — world."

24. "We believe in the doctrine of the freedom — press, and we therefore emphatically protest agai— suppression of Negro newspapers and periodic— various parts of the world, and call upon Negroes — where to employ all available means to prevent — suppression."

25. "We further demand free speech universal — all men."

OWNED BY: BLACK STAR LINE LTD.

31. "We declare that the teaching in any scho— teachers to our boys and girls, that the alien r— —perior to the Negro race, is an insult to the —— people of the world."

AFRICA THE LAND OF OPPORTUNITY

obstruc— their

NATIONAL HEREOS : *The Fight For Independence*

"Our success educationally, industrially and politically is based upon the protection of a nation founded by ourselves." - Marcus Garvey Sr.

Marcus Mosiah Garvey Sr.
(b. Aug. 17, 1887 – d. June 10, 1940)

Marcus Mosiah Garvey was born on August 17, 1887, in Saint Ann's Bay. Garvey took an apprenticeship in the print trade as a teenager in Kingston before traveling to Costa Rica, Panama, and England. Returning to Jamaica in 1914, he started the Universal Negro Improvement Association (UNIA). As the founder and first President-General of the UNIA, Garvey moved to the United States and established a UNIA branch in Harlem in 1916.

As an activist and journalist Garvey emphasized the emancipation of Africans and people of the African diaspora from European colonial rule and systems. Garvey preached unity, empowerment, development of businesses, and trade between black nations across the world. In 1919 he became President of the Black Star Line, a shipping and passenger company he established to transport goods and people between North America and Africa. His powerful words and actions quickly gained him a very large following.

The UNIA grew rapidly, establishing 25 branches in the United States in 2 years. As well as divisions in the West Indies, Central America, and Africa. This rapid growth caught the attention of the US government and the FBI. In January of 1922, Garvey was charged with multiple counts of mail fraud. He was convicted in 1923 and deported back to Jamaica in 1927.

In 1929 Garvey started the People's Political Party, Jamaica's first modern political party. In 1935 Garvey moved to London where he continued his work as an activist and political leader. Marcus Mosiah Garvey Sr. died in London on June 10th, 1940. In 1964 his body was exhumed and returned to Jamaica for reburial in Kingston's National Heroes Park.

Today Garvey is viewed as Jamaica's most influential figure. His principles and the crowning of Haile Selassie I as Emperor of Ethiopia became the foundation of Rastafari. In the United States Garvey is viewed as the father of the Black Nationalist movement and Pan-Africanism. Marcus Mosiah Garvey Sr. was conferred with the Order of National Hero in 1969. In 2012, Jamaica declared August 17th as Marcus Garvey Day.

NATIONAL HEREOS : *The Fight For Independence*

Sir William Alexander Clarke Bustamante
(b. Feb 24, 1884 – d. Aug 6, 1977)

Born as Alexander Clarke on February 24th, 1884 to Mary and Robert Constantine Clarke in Blenheim, Hanover. He took the surname Bustamante in honor of a Spaniard who adopted him and took him to Spain where he attended school. In 1932, he returned to Jamaica and immediately was an outspoken activist against colonial rules in Jamaica. He frequently wrote letters to the Daily Gleaner newspaper in defense of the poor working class of Jamaica. In 1937 he was elected treasurer of the Jamaica Workers' Union (JWU). He was the spokesman for striking workers during the 1938 labor rebellion. After the labor riots ended he started the Bustamante Industrial Trade Union in 1938. In 1940, he was imprisoned for 17 months on charges of subversive activities.

In 1943, Bustamante formed the Jamaica Labour Party in opposition his cousin Norman Manley's People's National Party. In 1947 and 1948, he served as mayor of Kingston. He was elected as Jamaica's first Chief Minister in 1953. Bustamante was also knighted by Queen Elizabeth in 1955 for his public services in Jamaica.

On August 6th, 1962, Jamaica gained independence from the United Kingdom. Sir Alexander Bustamante became the first Prime Minister of Jamaica in 1962. He held the position until 1965 when he suffered a stroke and withdrew from public service. His deputy, Donald Sangster finished his term as Prime Minister. In 1969, Bustamante was awarded the Order of National Hero (ONH). Sir Alexander Clarke Bustamante died on August 6th, 1977.

NATIONAL HEREOS : *The Fight For Independence*

Norman Washington Manley
(b. July 4, 1893 – d. Sept. 2, 1969)

Norman Washington Manley was born in Roxborough, Manchester, on July 4th, 1893. A Rhodes Scholar at Jamaica College, Manley became one of Jamaica's leading lawyers in the 1920s. He was an activist, athlete, and soldier in the Royal Field Artillery during World War I. He married Edna Manley in 1921 the two had two children; Douglas Manley and Michael Manley. In September 1938, Manley launched the People's National Party (PNP). He volunteered as a legal advocate for the workers during the 1938 labor rebellion. Manley advocated for the Universal Adult Suffrage that was ultimately approved in 1944. As a member of the West Indies Federation, he advocated for Jamaica's Independence into self-government.

Manley became Jamaica's 2nd Chief Minister in February of 1955. A position he held until August of 1959 when he was elected Jamaica's first Premier. As premier, Manley helped to develop a stronger governing system in Jamaica. Due to health issues, Manley retired from politics in 1969. He died later that year, on September 2nd, 1969. On October 18th, 1969 as per the order of the Jamaica Government, Norman Washington Manley was awarded the Order of National Hero.

Chief Ministers of Jamaica

1.

Sir Alexander Bustamante
Jamaica's first Chief Ministers
Term: 1953 to 1955 (JLP)

2.

Norman Manley
Term: 1955 to 1959 (PNP)

Prime Ministers of Jamaica

1.
Sir Alexander Bustamante
Term: 1962 to 1967

2.
Sir Donald Sangster
Term: 1967 Feb. to April

3.
Hugh Shearer
Term: 1967 to 1972

4. Michael Manley
Terms: 1972 - 1980
1989 - 1992

5.
Edward Seaga
Term: 1980 - 1989

6.
Percival J. Patterson
Term: 1992 - 2005

7.
Portia Simpson-Miller
Terms: 2005 - 2007,
2012 - 2016

8.
Orette Bruce Golding
Term: 2007 - 2011

9.
Andrew Holness
Terms: 2011 - 2012
2016 - Incumbent

Individuals of Great Merit

The iron hand of oppression daily endeavours to keep the slaves in the ignorance to which it has reduced them.
— William Knibb

William Knibb, (Baptist minister)

Reverend William Knibb, (b. Sept. 7, 1803 – d. Nov. 15, 1845)

William Knibb was an English Baptist minister and missionary in Jamaica. He was the first white man to receive the Jamaican Order of Merit in 1988 for his antislavery work in the early 1800s. Knibb began work in Jamaica in 1825 as the schoolmaster of the Baptist mission school in Kingston, before moving to Savanna-la-Mar in 1828. In 1830 he became the minister of the Baptist church at Falmouth. He remained there as minister until his death on November 15, 1845.

Individuals of Great Merit

Mary Jane Seacole, (b. 1805 – d. 1881)

Mary Jane Seacole was a British-Jamaican businesswoman, nurse, and explorer who set up the "British Hotel" behind enemy lines during the Crimean War. She provided comfortable quarters for treating the sick and wounded. In her autobiography, *Wonderful Adventures of Mrs. Seacole in Many Lands* (1857), one of the earliest known autobiographies by a black woman. In it, she documents her travels around the world. She was awarded the Jamaican Order 0f Merit in 1991. In 2004 she was voted the greatest black Briton.

Individuals of Great Merit: *Medicine & Science*

Dr. Cicely Williams

Dr. Thomas Phillip

Dr. Cicely Delphine Williams, (b. 1893 - d. 1992)

Cicely Delphine Williams was born in Kew Park, Darliston Westmoreland, Jamaica on December 2, 1893. Cicely Williams discovered the disease kwashiorkor, a severe form of protein malnutrition, fatal if not treated promptly. She identified the cause, studied it, and developed preventions and a cure. She was awarded the Jamaica Order of Merit in recognition of distinguished work in the area of Maternal and Child Health in 1975. Dr. Cicely Williams died in Oxford, England in 1992 at the age of 98.

Dr. Thomas Phillip Lecky, (b. 1904 - d. 1994)

Thomas Phillip Lecky, the pioneer Jamaican Scientist, was born on December 31, 1904, in Portland. Dr. Lecky studied agriculture and agricultural Science. He dedicated his life as a scientist to developing better breeding techniques and breeds of livestock more suitable to tropical climate. Dr. Lecky's research resulted in the first breed of indigenous Jamaican cattle, the Jamaica Hope in 1951. Further crossbreeding experiments, resulted in the Jamaican Red and Jamaican Black cattle breeds. Dr. Lecky's work became the standard for breeders in tropical climates around the world. He received the Order of the British Empire in 1958 for his achievements and was the first recipient of the Norman Manley Award for Excellence in 1970. Dr. Lecky was also awarded Jamaica's highest civilian honor, the Order of Merit. Dr. Lecky died in 1994 at the age of 90.

Individuals of Great Merit: *The Arts*

Edna Manley, (Artist)

Ralston Nettleford, (Professor)

Edna Swithenbank Manley, (b. March 1, 1900 – d. February 2, 1987)

Edna Manley, the mother of Jamaican art, was one of the most accomplished sculptors and art educators in Jamaica. The wife of Norman Manley and mother of former Prime Minister Michael Manley. She was influential in the forming of the Jamaica School of Art and Craft in 1950. Later renamed the Edna Manley College of the Visual and Performing Arts in 1995 in her honor. She received many awards and honors in her lifetime, including the Jamaica Order of Merit. Edna Manley died on February 2, 1987.

Ralston Milton Nettleford, (February 3, 1933 - February 2, 2010)

Ralston Rex Nettleford was an international scholar, cultural ambassador, author, choreographer, critic, educator, and Vice-Chancellor Emeritus of the University of the West Indies (UWI). He received the Jamaican Order of Merit in 1975 and the Gold Musgrave Medal in 1981 for his cultural and scholarly achievements. Ralston Rex Nettleford was pronounced dead in Washington DC on February 2, 2010, after suffering a heart attack.

Individuals of Great Merit: *The Arts*

Rt. Hon. Dr. Louise Simone Bennett-Coverley, (b. 1919 – d. 2006)

Louise Bennett-Coverley (Miss Lou) was a poet, folklorist, performer, writer, historian, and educator born on September 7, 1919, in Kingston. In 1945, she was awarded a British Council scholarship to the Royal Academy of Dramatic Art (RADA) in London, England. In her work and life, Miss Lou displayed great pride in Jamaican history, culture, and dialect. Miss Lou taught speech and drama at Excelsior High School. She was also a radio and television personality. Miss Lou was known as a cultural ambassador for Jamaica. She received many accolades and honors for work during her lifetime including Member of the Most Excellent Order of the British Empire in 1960, the Norman Manley Award for Excellence in 1972, Order of Jamaica in 1974, the Musgrave Medal in 1978, Honorary degree of Doctor of Letters from the University of the West Indies in 1983, Honorary degree of Doctor of Letters from York University, Toronto Canada in 1998, and the Jamaican Order of Merit in 2001. Miss Lou died on July 26, 2006.

Individuals of Great Merit: Reggae

Bob Marley, *(Reggae Musician)*

Peter Tosh, *(Reggae Musician)*

Robert Nesta Marley (Bob Marley), (b. Feb 6, 1945 – d. May 11, 1981)

Bob Marley is recognized worldwide as one of the greatest musicians of all time. Marley began his music career in 1963 as a member of The Wailers. As a solo artist Marley established himself as a music icon. He is estimated to have sold over 75 million records worldwide. In 1977, Marley was diagnosed with acral lentiginous melanoma. He died as a result of that illness in 1981. Marley was awarded the Jamaica Order of Merit in 1981. His greatest hits album *Legend* released in 1984 is the highest-selling reggae album of all time. Marley was inducted into the Rock and Roll Hall of Fame in 1994.

Winston Hubert McIntosh (Peter Tosh), (b. Oct. 19, 1944 – d. Sept. 11, 1987)

Peter Tosh was a Rastafarian reggae musician. Who along with Bob Marley and Bunny Wailer formed the legendary reggae band the Wailers in 1963. Tosh remained apart of the Wailers until 1976 when he embarked on his solo career. Tosh released 7 solo albums, won a Grammy Award for Best Reggae Performance in 1987 for No Nuclear War. Peter Tosh was murdered on September 11, 1987, during a home invasion. Tosh was posthumously awarded the Jamaica Order of Merit in 2012.

Individuals of Great Merit: *Reggae*

Bunny Wailer, *(Reggae Musician)*

Jimmy Cliff, *(Reggae Musician)*

Neville O'Riley Livingston (Bunny Wailer), (b. April 10, 1947)

Neville O'Riley Livingston, better known as Bunny Wailer or Bunny Livingston is a three-time Grammy award-winning reggae music icon. One of the founding member of the legendary reggae group The Wailers along with Bob Marley and Peter Tosh. Bunny Wailer won the Grammy for Best Reggae Album in 1991 for *Time Will Tell*, 1995 for *Crucial! Roots Classics*, and 1997 for *Hall of Fame*. In 2012 he received Jamaica's fifth highest honor, the Order of Jamaica. In October of 2017 he was awarded the Order of Merit.

James Chambers (Jimmy Cliff), (b. April 1, 1948)

James Chambers, born April 1, 1948, known better as Jimmy Cliff, is a Jamaican ska and reggae musician, singer, and actor. Jimmy Cliff starred in the 1972 film The Harder They Come, which helped to popularize reggae music across the world. Jimmy Cliff became a platinum-selling musician. Jimmy Cliff was awarded the Jamaican Order of Merit on October 20, 2003. In 2010 Jimmy Cliff was inducted into the Rock and Roll Hall of Fame.

Individuals of Great Merit: *Reggae*

The Cool Ruler (Gregory Isaacs) c. 2018

Gregory Anthony Isaacs, (b. July 15, 1951 – d. October 25, 2010)

Gregory Isaacs was one of the most prolific and exquisite vocalist in reggae music. Isaacs recored over 70 original studio albums between 1975 and 2010. Isaacs have been apart of over 500 albums to date. Isaacs was nominated for four Grammy, including 2011 for his final studio album *Isaacs Meets Isaac*, with King Isaac in 2010. Gregory Isaacs died of lung cancer on October 25, 2010 at his home in London.

RASTAFARI

RASTAFARI: *The Movement*

King & Queen (Lion & Lioness)

Rastafari is an Africa-centred spiritual movement that developed in Jamaica in the 1930s, following the coronation of Haile Selassie I as Emperor of Ethiopia in 1930. Rastafari utilizes the principles of Marcus Garvey, Haile Selassie I along with a natural way of life, ital diet, and growing one's hair into dreadlocks. Religious leader Leonard P Howell is credited as the founding member of the Rastafari movement alongside Joseph Hibbert, Archibald Dunkley, and Robert Hinds.

With the growing popularity of reggae music Rastafari became one of the most influential cultural and spiritual movements of the 20th century. Influential figures of the movement are Bob Marley, Peter Tosh, and Mutabaruka to name a few.

Mutabaruka, (Dub poet, Social Activist)
b. 1952 in Kingston, Jamaica

Competitive Excellence in Athletics

George Alphonso Headley, (May 30, 1909 – November 30, 1983)

George Headley was a West Indian cricketer who played for Jamaica and the West Indies. Born in Panama, Headley was taken to Jamaica at the age of 10, where he fell in love with cricket. Headley made his professional cricket debut in 1930. Headley was the first of the great black batsmen to emerge from Jamaica and the West Indies. In 22 Tests, Headley scored 2190 runs, including 10 centuries. He is considered one of the greatest cricketers of all time. Headley led the way for Jamaican cricketers like Michael Holding, James (Jimmy) Adams, Courtney Walsh, and Christopher Gayle to name a few.

Competitive Excellence in Athletics

Arthur Stanley Wint *Herb McKenley*

Arthur Stanley Wint, (b. May 25, 1920 – d. Oct. 19, 1992)
Herbert Henry "Herb" McKenley, (b. July 10, 1922 – d. Nov. 26, 2007)

The Hon. Herbert "Herb" McKenley was a Jamaican sprint, who competed at the 1948 and 1952 Olympics in six events. Herb was the only sprinter to make the final in all three sprinting events, the 100m, 200m, and 400m in the 1948 Olympics. He finished second in 400m, behind teammate Arthur Wint. Wint became Jamaica's first Olympic gold medalist. Wint finished his Olympic career with two gold medals and two silver medals. Herb McKenley finished his Olympic career with one gold medal and three silver medals. McKenley coached the Jamaican national team from 1954 to 1973. Jamaica awarded McKenley The Order of Merit in 2004.

Competitive Excellence in Athletics

Deon Hemmings (Olympic track star)

Deon Hemmings, (b. Oct 9, 1968)

Deon Hemmings is Jamaica's first Olympic gold medalist. She won the 400m Hurdles at the 1996 Olympics breaking the then Olympic record. Hemmings accomplishment was an inspiration to future Jamaican track stars like Veronica Campbell Brown, Shelly-Ann Fraser-Pryce, and Elain Thompson.

Shelly-Ann Fraser-Pryce, (b. Dec 27, 1986)

Shelly-Ann Fraser-Pryce is the first Jamaican woman to win 100m gold at the Olympics. She won the 100m title at the 2008 and 2012 Olympics. She became the first woman in history to win 100m medals at three consecutive Olympics when she took the bronze medal in the 2016 Rio Olympic Games.

Shelly-Ann Fraser-Pryce (Greatest 100m sprinter of all time)

Competitive Excellence in Athletics

Usain St Leo Bolt, (b. August 21, 1986)

Usain Bolt is an eight-time Olympic gold medalist. He is the world record holder in the 100m, 200m, and 4 × 100m relays. The fastest man in the world and the most dominant sprinter of all time. He is the most successful athlete in World Championships history. He is the first athlete to win four World Championship titles in the 200m. Bolt was the first sprinter to run under 9.7 seconds in the 100m, a record he would break in 2009 when completed the 100m in 9.58 seconds at the World Championships in Berlin. Bolt also holds the 200m world record, setting 19.30 in 2008 and 19.19 in 2009. Bolt retired from sprinting in 2017. Bolt is highly considered the greatest sprinter of all time.

Usain Bolt
(Fastest sprinter of all time)

The future of Jamaica is what we make it.

"Up, you mighty race, accomplish what you will."
- Marcus Garvey Sr.

Made in United States
North Haven, CT
30 March 2023